C000090654

Cook's Corner

Creative
Cocktails

igloobooks

igloobooks

Published in 2018
by Igloo Books Ltd
Cottage Farm
Sywell
NN6 0BJ
www.igloobooks.com

STA002 0218
2 4 6 8 10 9 7 5 3 1
ISBN: 978-1-78810-187-5

Cover designed by Nicholas Gage
Interiors designed by Simon Parker
Edited by Jasmin Peppiatt

Printed and manufactured in China

Cook's Corner

Creative
Cocktails

Contents

Cook's Corner

Creative
Cocktails

Long Island iced tea

SERVES: 1 | PREP TIME: 5 MINUTES

INGREDIENTS

½ shot vodka

½ shot tequila

½ shot white rum

½ shot gin

½ shot triple sec

½ shot lime juice

½ shot lemon juice

7 ice cubes

1 lemon wedge

1 sprig rosemary

cola

METHOD

1. Put the vodka, tequila, rum, gin, triple sec, lime juice and lemon juice in a cocktail shaker with six of the ice cubes.

2. Shake vigorously for 1 minute, then strain into a rocks glass.

3. Add the lemon wedge, rosemary and remaining ice cube, then top up with cola.

Watermelon rum

SERVES: 1 | PREP TIME: 5 MINUTES

INGREDIENTS

3 handfuls watermelon chunks, deseeded

1 tsp sugar

1 shot lime juice

1 shot lemon juice

1 shot white rum

ice cubes

soda water

TO SERVE:

a handful of mint leaves

1 slice lemon

METHOD

1. Put the watermelon chunks through a juicer, as per the manufacturer's instructions.

2. Mix the sugar, lemon juice and lime juice together in a glass.

3. Add the rum, watermelon juice and desired amount of ice cubes.

4. Top up with soda water.

5. Serve with mint leaves and a slice of lemon.

Mojito

SERVES: 1 | PREP TIME: 5 MINUTES

INGREDIENTS

10 mint leaves

1 tsp sugar syrup

1 tsp sugar

1 shot white rum

1 shot lime juice

1 lime, cut into small chunks

5 ice cubes

soda water

METHOD

1. Mash the mint, sugar syrup and sugar together in a glass or jar, ensuring the mint leaves are crushed to release the flavour.

2. Add the rum, lime juice, lime chunks and ice.

3. Top up with soda water and stir well with a cocktail mixer.

4. Serve immediately with extra ice, if desired.

Mellow lemon

MAKES: 1 LITRE | PREP TIME: 5 MINUTES

●●●●●●●●●●●●●●●●●●●●●●●●●●●●

INGREDIENTS

ice cubes

250 ml / 9 fl. oz / 1 cup vodka

150 ml / 5 ½ fl. oz / ⅔ cup limoncello

250 ml / 9 fl. oz / 1 cup fresh lemon juice

4 shots sugar syrup

2 lemons, sliced

1 small bunch mint

chilled mineral water

METHOD

1. Half fill a large jug with ice cubes.

2. Add the vodka, limoncello, lemon juice, sugar syrup, lemons and mint.

3. Stir for 1 minute.

4. Top up the jug with mineral water to taste.

5. Pour into individual glasses and serve immediately.

Orange fizz

SERVES: 1 | PREP TIME: 10 MINUTES

INGREDIENTS

salt

ice

½ orange

35 ml / 1 ¼ fl. oz gin

1 tbsp lemon juice

2 tsp orange liqueur

1 tsp simple syrup

2 drops of bitters

soda water

orange wedge and rosemary sprigs to garnish

METHOD

1. Wet the rim of a lowball glass and dip into the salt.

2. Half fill the glass with ice, to chill.

3. Juice the orange and set aside.

4. Add the gin, lemon, liqueur, syrup and bitters to a cocktail shaker and half fill with ice.

5. Shake well and strain into the prepared glass.

6. Top up with the orange juice and then soda water

7. Garnish with an orange wedge and a sprig of rosemary.

Tom Collins

SERVES: 2 | PREP TIME: 5 MINUTES

INGREDIENTS

4 shots gin

2 shots fresh lemon juice

1 shot sugar syrup

8 ice cubes

crushed ice

soda water

lemon wedges, to serve

METHOD

1. Put the gin in a cocktail shaker with the lemon juice, sugar syrup and ice cubes Shake vigorously for 1 minute.

2. Fill two Collins glasses with crushed ice and strain the cocktail over the top.

3. Top up with soda water.

4. Garnish with lemon wedges and serve.

Cosmopolitan

SERVES: 1 | PREP TIME: 5 MINUTES

INGREDIENTS

2 ice cubes

1 shot vodka

1 shot lime juice

1 shot triple sec

3 shots cranberry juice

TO SERVE:

1 wedge of watermelon or lime

sprig of mint

METHOD

1. Put the ice into a cocktail shaker.

2. Add the vodka, lime juice, triple sec and cranberry juice over the ice, then shake for 20 seconds.

3. Pour into a martini glass.

4. Serve immediately, garnished with a wedge of watermelon or lime as preferred and a sprig of mint.

Mai tai

SERVES: 1 | PREP TIME: 5 MINUTES

INGREDIENTS

ice cubes

½ shot almond syrup

½ shot sugar syrup

½ shot dark rum

1 shot light rum

2 shots orange curaçao

fresh lime juice

TO SERVE:

1 cherry

1 pineapple wedge

2 spikes cut from the pineapple crown

METHOD

1. Put the ice into a cocktail shaker.

2. Pour the almond syrup, sugar syrup, dark rum, light rum and 1 shot of the orange Curaçao over the ice in the shaker, then shake for 20 seconds.

3. Pour into a glass, top up with lime juice and pour over the second shot of orange Curaçao.

4. Serve immediately, garnished with a cherry, wedge of pineapple and a couple of the spikes from the pineapple crown.

Vodka zing

SERVES: 1 | PREP TIME: 5 MINUTES

●●●●●●●●●●●●●●●●●●●●●●●●●●●

INGREDIENTS

5 ice cubes

1 shot vodka

½ shot lime juice

½ shot lemon juice

cloudy lemonade

TO SERVE:

1 lime slice

sprig of mint

METHOD

1. Put the ice cubes into a cocktail shaker.

2. Pour the vodka and citrus juices into the cocktail shaker over the ice and shake for 10 seconds.

3. Pour the mixture into a glass and top up with cloudy lemonade.

4. Serve garnished with a lime slice and a sprig of mint.

Irish coffee

SERVES: 1 | PREP TIME: 5-8 MINUTES

INGREDIENTS

2 tsp brown sugar

1 tsp coffee granules

150 ml / 5 fl. oz near-boiling water

2 shots Irish cream liqueur

whipped cream

TO SERVE:

1 tsp cocoa powder

METHOD

1. Stir the sugar and coffee granules together in a thick, heatproof glass with 150 ml of near-boiling water.

2. Stir well to ensure it is mixed.

3. Add the Irish cream liqueur and stir again.

4. Float the whipped cream on the top and serve immediately, sprinkled with cocoa powder if desired.

Rosemary vodka

SERVES: 2 | PREP TIME: 5 MINUTES

INGREDIENTS

5 sprigs of rosemary

4 shots vodka

2 shots lemon juice

2 shots lime juice

1 shot sugar syrup

8 ice cubes

10 slices cucumber

2 slices lemon, halved

chilled mineral water

METHOD

1. Muddle three of the rosemary sprigs in the base of a cocktail shaker.

2. Add the vodka, citrus juices, sugar syrup and ice. Shake vigorously for 1 minute.

3. Add the cucumber, sliced lemon and remaining rosemary to two small glass bottles and strain in the cocktail.

4. Top up with mineral water to taste.

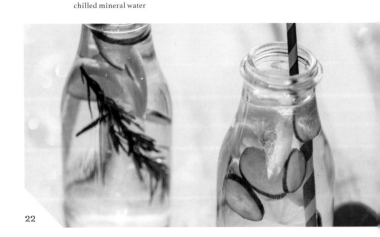

Orgasm

SERVES: 1 | PREP TIME: 5 MINUTES

INGREDIENTS

a handful of ice cubes

2 shots Irish cream liqueur

1 shot amaretto

1 shot coffee liqueur

2 shots cream

4 shots milk

METHOD

1. Put the ice into a cocktail shaker.

2. Pour all of the ingredients over the ice in the shaker, then shake for 20 seconds.

3. Strain into a glass, adding more ice if desired.

Pick me up

SERVES: 1 | PREP TIME: 5 MINUTES

INGREDIENTS

1 shot brandy

1 shot orange juice, chilled

1 shot peach juice, chilled

Champagne

a handful of ice cubes

METHOD

1. Pour the brandy and fruit juices into a flute glass.

2. Gently add the ice cubes.

3. Top up with Champagne, being careful that it does not overflow.

4. Stir thoroughly then serve immediately.

Russian mojito

SERVES: 1 | PREP TIME: 10 MINUTES

•••••••••••••••••••••••••

INGREDIENTS

½ lime, cut into wedges

1 tsp caster (superfine) sugar

8 mint leaves

crushed ice

50 ml / 1 ¾ fl. oz / ¼ cup citrus vodka

soda water

METHOD

1. Muddle the lime, sugar and mint in the bottom of a highball glass.

2. Fill the glass up to three quarters with crushed ice.

3. Add the vodka and stir to combine.

4. Top up with soda water.

Piña colada

SERVES: 1 | PREP TIME: 5 MINUTES

INGREDIENTS

4 ice cubes

2 shots white rum

5 shots pineapple juice

2 shots coconut cream

TO SERVE:

sprig of mint

1 pineapple wedge, peeled

1 vanilla pod

METHOD

1. Put the ice cubes into a cocktail shaker.

2. Pour the rest of the ingredients over the ice in the shaker and shake for 30 seconds.

3. Pour into a tall glass.

4. Serve garnished with a mint sprig, pineapple wedge and vanilla pod.

Fruity cocktail

SERVES: 4 | PREP TIME: 5 MINUTES

INGREDIENTS

ice cubes

1 orange, cut into small chunks

2 apples, cut into small chunks

2 lemons, cut into wedges

2 limes, cut into wedges

a handful of mint leaves

5 shots fruit cup

lemonade

METHOD

1. Put ice into the jug and add the chopped fruit, mint leaves and fruit cup.

2. Top up with lemonade.

3. Gently stir the mixture using a cocktail stirrer, ensuring it is thoroughly mixed together.

4. Pour into individual glasses with more ice.

5. Serve immediately.

Lemon mojito

SERVES: 1 | PREP TIME: 5 MINUTES

INGREDIENTS

1 tsp caster (superfine) sugar

a handful of fresh mint

½ lemon, sliced

50 ml / 1 ¾ fl. oz / ¼ cup golden rum

soda water

crushed ice

METHOD

1. Place the sugar and mint into a tall glass and muddle together.

2. Add the lemon and rum and stir together.

3. Top up the glass with soda water and ice.

Coco loco

SERVES: 1 | PREP TIME: 5 MINUTES

INGREDIENTS

ice

35 ml / 1 ¼ fl. oz spiced rum

35 ml / 1 ¼ fl. oz orange liqueur

½ lemon, juiced

cola

lemon slices to garnish

METHOD

1. Half fill a highball glass with ice.

2. Pour the rum, liqueur and lemon juice over the ice and stir.

3. Top the glass up with cola.

4. Garnish with lemon slices.

Fuzzy navel

SERVES: 1 | PREP TIME: 5 MINUTES

INGREDIENTS

ice

30 ml / 1 fl. oz peach schnapps

30 ml / 1 fl. oz vodka

orange juice

METHOD

1. Place the ice into a glass to chill it.

2. Pour the peach schnapps and vodka into the glass and stir.

3. Top up with orange juice.

Gin and tonic

SERVES: 1 | PREP TIME: 5 MINUTES

INGREDIENTS

150 ml / 5 fl. oz tonic water, chilled

2 shots gin

TO SERVE:

a handful of cucumber slices

½ lemon, thinly sliced

½ lime, thinly sliced

METHOD

1. Pour the chilled tonic water and gin into a glass.

2. Stir well.

3. Serve with several cucumber, lemon and lime slices.

4. For added flavour, add a sprig of rosemary or thyme if desired.

Tequila sunrise

SERVES: 1 | PREP TIME: 5 MINUTES

INGREDIENTS

6 ice cubes

2 shots tequila

orange juice

1 shot grenadine

TO SERVE:

1 cherry

1 orange slice

METHOD

1. Pour the tequila into a tall glass filled with the ice.

2. Top up with orange juice, but don't fill.

3. Pour the grenadine down the inside of the glass so it sinks to the bottom.

4. Garnish with a cherry and an orange slice.

5. Serve immediately.

Margarita

SERVES: 1 | PREP TIME: 5 MINUTES

INGREDIENTS

3 ice cubes

2 shots fresh lime juice

2 shots tequila

1 shot triple sec

a pinch of salt

TO SERVE:

salt, for the rim of the glass

1 lime slice

METHOD

1. Put the ice into a cocktail shaker.

2. Pour the rest of the ingredients over the ice in the shaker, then shake for 10 seconds.

3. Dip the rim of the margarita glass in water, then into a bowl of salt.

4. Pour the mixture into the glass, leaving the ice in the cocktail shaker.

5. Serve garnished with a lime slice.

Lime zinger

SERVES: 1 | PREP TIME: 5 MINUTES

• •

INGREDIENTS

ice cubes

2 shots lime juice

1 shot lime cordial

1 shot tequila

soda water

TO SERVE:

1 lime slice

extra ice cubes

METHOD

1. Put the ice into a cocktail shaker.

2. Pour the lime juice, lime cordial and tequila over the ice in the cocktail shaker, then shake for 10 seconds.

3. Strain the mixture into the glass, topping it up with soda water.

4. Serve garnished with a lime slice and extra ice cubes.

Peachsecco

SERVES: 1 | PREP TIME: 5 MINUTES

INGREDIENTS

2 shots white rum

3 shots peach iced tea, chilled

prosecco

TO SERVE:

a handful of raspberries, preferably frozen

a handful of peach wedges

METHOD

1. Pour the white rum and peach iced tea into the cocktail shaker, then shake for 10 seconds.

2. Pour into a glass and top up with prosecco.

3. Serve immediately, floating the raspberries and peach wedges in the cocktail.

All American fizz

SERVES: 1 | PREP TIME: 5 MINUTES

INGREDIENTS

2 handfuls strawberries

5 ice cubes

1 shot gin

1 shot brandy

1 shot lemon juice

½ shot grenadine

soda water

TO SERVE:

2 handfuls crushed ice

METHOD

1. Process the strawberries through a juicer according to the manufacturer's instructions.

2. Put the ice cubes into the cocktail shaker and pour over the strained strawberry juice, gin, brandy, lemon juice and grenadine.

3. Pour into a glass and top up with soda water.

4. Serve immediately with crushed ice.

Vodka sour

SERVES: 1 | PREP TIME: 5 MINUTES

INGREDIENTS

2 shots vodka

1 shot fresh lemon juice

¾ shot sugar syrup

8 ice cubes

1 slice lemon

METHOD

1. Put the vodka, lemon juice and sugar syrup in a cocktail shaker with six of the ice cubes.

2. Shake vigorously for 1 minute.

3. Wrap the lemon slice around the other two ice cubes and place in an old-fashioned glass.

4. Strain the cocktail into the glass and serve immediately.

Woo woo

SERVES: 1 | PREP TIME: 5 MINUTES

INGREDIENTS

5 ice cubes

1 shot peach schnapps

2 shots vodka

5 shots cranberry juice

TO SERVE:

1 lime slice

METHOD

1. Put the 5 ice cubes into the cocktail shaker.

2. Pour the peach schnapps and vodka over the ice in the shaker, then shake for at least 20 seconds.

3. Pour into a tall glass and top up with the cranberry juice.

4. Serve with a slice of lime.

Vodka martini

SERVES: 1 | PREP TIME: 5 MINUTES

INGREDIENTS

4 ice cubes

1 shot dry vermouth

2 shots vodka

2 olives

METHOD

1. Put the ice cubes into a cocktail shaker.

2. Pour the dry vermouth and vodka into the cocktail shaker over the ice and shake for 20 seconds.

3. Pour the mixture into a martini glass, leaving the ice in the cocktail shaker.

4. Thread 2 olives onto a cocktail stick and balance it on the side of the glass.

5. Serve immediately with extra olives, if desired.

Black Russian

SERVES: 1 | PREP TIME: 5 MINUTES

INGREDIENTS

4 ice cubes

1 shot coffee liqueur

1 shot vodka

cola

TO SERVE:

1 lime slice

METHOD

1. Put the ice into a cocktail shaker.

2. Add the coffee liqueur and vodka over the ice in the shaker, then shake for 10 seconds.

3. Pour into a glass and top up with cola.

4. Serve immediately, garnished with a slice of lime.

White Russian

SERVES: 1 | PREP TIME: 5 MINUTES

INGREDIENTS

1 large ice cube

2 shots vodka

1 shot coffee liqueur

4 shots cream

METHOD

1. Put the ice cube into the cocktail shaker.

2. Add the vodka and coffee liqueur over the ice in the shaker, then shake for 10 seconds.

3. Pour into a glass and gently pour in the cream.

4. Allow the ice to cool the cocktail for 2-3 minutes before drinking.

47

Frozen kiwi daiquiri

SERVES: 2 | PREP TIME: 5 MINUTES | FREEZING TIME: 2 HOURS

INGREDIENTS

3 kiwi fruit, peeled and sliced

1 banana, peeled and sliced

3 shots white rum

1 shot kiwi liqueur

1 shot fresh lime juice

6 ice cubes

2 cherries

METHOD

1. Reserve four slices of kiwi for the garnish. Spread the rest out on a baking tray with the banana and freeze for at least 2 hours. They can then be stored in a freezer bag for later use or used straight away.

2. Put the frozen fruit in a liquidizer with the rum, kiwi liqueur, lime juice and ice. Blend until very smooth.

3. Pour the cocktail into two glasses and garnish with kiwi slices and cherries threaded onto a skewer.

Bloody Mary

SERVES: 1 | PREP TIME: 5 MINUTES

INGREDIENTS

4 ice cubes

2 dashes Worcestershire sauce

1 dash hot sauce

1 shot vodka

1 dash lemon juice

150 ml / 5 fl. oz tomato juice

a pinch of sea salt

a pinch of black pepper

TO SERVE:

1 lime wedge

1 bacon rasher, fried until crispy

METHOD

1. Put the 4 ice cubes into the cocktail shaker.

2. Pour the Worcestershire sauce and hot sauce over the ice, then add the vodka, lemon juice and tomato juice.

3. Shake the cocktail shaker for at least 30 seconds.

4. Pour into a glass and add a pinch of salt and pepper.

5. Serve garnished with a small lime wedge and a rasher of fried bacon for decoration.

Watermelon woo woo

SERVES: 1 | PREP TIME: 5 MINUTES

INGREDIENTS

3 ice cubes

1 shot peach schnapps

1 shot vodka

2 shots cranberry juice

4 shots watermelon juice

TO SERVE:

1 lime slice

sprig of mint

a handful of crushed ice (optional)

METHOD

1. Put the ice into a cocktail shaker.

2. Pour the peach schnapps and vodka over the ice in the shaker, then shake for at least 20 seconds.

3. Pour into a glass and top up with the cranberry juice and watermelon juice.

4. Serve immediately, garnished with a slice of lime and a sprig of mint.

5. If desired, top up with crushed ice.

Piña berry colada

SERVES: 1 | PREP TIME: 5 MINUTES

INGREDIENTS

a handful of blueberries, washed

a handful of blackberries, washed

a handful of crushed ice

1 shot white rum

2 shots coconut cream

pineapple juice

TO SERVE:

sprig of mint

METHOD

1. Put the blueberries and blackberries in a blender and whizz for 30 seconds.

2. Put the crushed ice into a cocktail shaker.

3. Pour the blended berries, white rum and coconut cream over the crushed ice in the shaker and shake for at least 30 seconds.

4. Pour into a glass and top up with pineapple juice.

5. Serve garnished with a sprig of mint.

Screwdriver

SERVES: 2 | PREP TIME: 5 MINUTES

INGREDIENTS

ice

60 ml / 2 fl. oz / ¼ cup vodka

120 ml / 4 fl. oz / ½ cup fresh orange juice

soda water

METHOD

1. Half fill two lowball glasses with ice.

2. Divide the vodka between the two glasses.

3. Top up the fresh orange juice and then soda water.

Greyhound spritz

SERVES: 2 | PREP TIME: 10 MINUTES

•••••••••••••••••••••••••••

INGREDIENTS

1 grapefruit

ice

100 ml / 3 ½ fl. oz / ½ cup grapefruit vodka

250 ml / 9 fl. oz / 1 cup soda water

METHOD

1. Slice the grapefruit in half and juice three quarters of the fruit. Cut the rest into wedges.

2. Half fill highball glasses with ice.

3. Pour the grapefruit juice and vodka into the glasses evenly.

4. Stir to combine and top up with the soda water. Garnish with the grapefruit wedges.

Espresso white Russian

SERVES: 1 | PREP TIME: 10 MINUTES

INGREDIENTS

ice

25 ml / 1 fl. oz espresso vodka

25 ml / 1 fl. oz Irish coffee cream liqueur

1 espresso

200 ml / 7 fl. oz / ¾ cup full fat milk

whipped cream

chocolate cookie to garnish

METHOD

1. Three quarters fill a mixing glass with ice and add the vodka, Irish coffee liqueur and espresso before stirring to combine.

2. Half fill a tall glass with ice and strain the vodka mixture into this.

3. Top up with the milk and stir.

4. Top with the whipped cream and cookie

Starlust

SERVES: 1 | PREP TIME: 5 MINUTES

INGREDIENTS

2 ice cubes

3 shots pineapple juice

1 shot vodka

1 tsp sugar syrup

2 pineapple wedges, peeled

1 star fruit, finely sliced and de-seeded

soda water

TO SERVE:

sprig of mint

METHOD

1. Put the ice cubes into a cocktail shaker.

2. Put the pineapple juice, vodka, sugar syrup, pineapple wedges and star fruit in the cocktail shaker, then shake well for 20 seconds, allowing the flavour to come out of the fruit.

3. Pour the cocktail into a glass and top up with soda water.

4. Serve garnished with a sprig of mint.

Purple lagoon

SERVES: 1 | PREP TIME: 5 MINUTES

INGREDIENTS

4 ice cubes

2 shots vodka

2 shots blackberry cordial

lemonade

a handful of blackberries

TO SERVE:

1 lemon slice

sprig of mint

METHOD

1. Put the ice cubes into a cocktail shaker.

2. Pour the vodka and blackberry cordial over the ice in the shaker, then shake for 10 seconds.

3. Pour into a glass and top up with lemonade.

4. Add the handful of blackberries and lemon slice.

5. Serve immediately, garnished with a sprig of mint.

Harvey Wallbanger

SERVES: 1 | PREP TIME: 5 MINUTES

INGREDIENTS

3 ice cubes

1 shot vodka

½ shot lemon juice

fresh orange juice, strained

1 shot herbal liqueur

METHOD

1. Put the ice cubes into a glass.

2. Add the vodka and lemon juice, then top up with orange juice.

3. Pour the herbal liqueur into the mixture.

4. Serve immediately.

Sangria

SERVES: 6 | PREP TIME: 5 MINUTES

INGREDIENTS

10 ice cubes

1 bottle red wine

1 orange, cut into wedges

1 lemon, cut into wedges

2 tbsp sugar

3 shots brandy

300 ml / 10 fl. oz soda water

TO SERVE:

1 lime slice - additional fruit to taste (optional)

METHOD

1. Put the ice cubes into a large jug and pour in the red wine.

2. Squeeze the juice from the orange and lemon wedges into the jug then add the wedges themselves.

3. Add the sugar, brandy and soda water.

4. Stir well and pour into individual glasses.

5. Serve immediately.

Mojitwhoa

SERVES: 1 | PREP TIME: 5 MINUTES

INGREDIENTS

10 mint leaves or 5 mint sprigs

1 tsp sugar

2 shots white rum

2 shots lime juice

1 lime, cut into small chunks

3 shots apple juice, chilled

½ apple, cut into thin slices

5 ice cubes

soda water

METHOD

1. Mash the mint and sugar together in a glass or jar.

2. Add the rum, lime juice, lime chunks, apple juice, apple slices and ice.

3. Top up with soda water, stir well and serve immediately.

Blue Hawaiian

SERVES: 3 | PREP TIME: 5-8 MINUTES

INGREDIENTS

5 ice cubes

6 shots light rum

2 shots coconut milk

3 shots blue curaçao

pineapple juice

TO SERVE:

3 lemon slices

2 handfuls ice cubes

METHOD

1. Put 5 ice cubes into the cocktail shaker.

2. Pour the light rum, coconut milk and 2 shots of the blue curaçao and the pineapple juice over the ice in the cocktail shaker, then shake for 30 seconds.

3. Pour the mixture into a large jug.

4. Top up with coconut milk.

5. Pour the final shot of blue curaçao down the inside of the jug so that it sits at the bottom and gives a gradient effect.

6. Top up the jug with more ice cubes and some lemon slices.

7. Serve immediately.

Frozen tropical daiquiri

SERVES: 2 | PREP TIME: 5 MINUTES | FREEZING TIME: 2 HOURS

INGREDIENTS

½ ripe mango, peeled and cubed

1 banana, peeled and sliced

4 shots white rum

1 shot orange liqueur

1 orange, juiced

1 shot fresh lime juice

8 ice cubes

1 passion fruit, halved

METHOD

1. Spread out the mango on a baking tray with the banana and freeze for at least 2 hours. They can then be stored in a freezer bag for later use or used straight away.

2. Put the frozen fruit in a liquidizer with the rum, liqueur, fruit juices and ice. Blend until very smooth.

3. Pour the cocktail into two glasses and scoop the passion fruit seeds on top.

Rainbow punch

SERVES: 1 | PREP TIME: 5 MINUTES

INGREDIENTS

4 ice cubes

2 shots grapefruit juice

3 shots cranberry juice

2 shots orange juice

1 shot lemon juice

1 shot vodka

a dash grenadine

a handful of redcurrants or cranberries

1 lemon slice

METHOD

1. Put 2 ice cubes into the cocktail shaker.

2. Pour the fruit juices, vodka and grenadine over the ice cubes in the cocktail shaker, then shake for 20 seconds.

3. Strain into a glass and add the remaining 2 ice cubes, the redcurrants and a slice of lemon.

Extra pineapple piña colada

SERVES: 1 | PREP TIME: 5 MINUTES

INGREDIENTS

a handful of pineapple chunks

4 ice cubes

1 shot white rum

5 shots pineapple juice

2 shots coconut cream

TO SERVE:

1 pineapple wedge

METHOD

1. Put the pineapple chunks in a blender and whizz for 20 seconds. Pour into a glass to fill the bottom half.

2. Put the ice cubes into a cocktail shaker.

3. Pour the white rum, pineapple juice and coconut cream over the ice in the shaker and shake for at least 30 seconds.

4. Pour gently into a glass to fill it to the top, leaving the blended pineapple chunks to sit in the bottom of the glass.

5. Serve garnished with a pineapple wedge.

Blue lagoon

SERVES: 1 | PREP TIME: 5 MINUTES

INGREDIENTS

2 ice cubes

2 shots vodka

1 shot blue Curaçao

lemonade

TO SERVE:

1 lemon slice

METHOD

1. Put the ice cubes into a cocktail shaker.

2. Pour the vodka and blue Curaçao over the ice in the shaker, then shake for 10 seconds.

3. Leaving the ice cubes in the shaker, pour the mixture into a glass and top up with lemonade.

4. Serve immediately, garnished with a slice of lemon.

Marma-rita

SERVES: 1 | PREP TIME: 5 MINUTES

INGREDIENTS

1 tsp salt

1 tsp caster (superfine) sugar

1 lemon wedge

2 shots tequila reposado

1 shot triple sec

1 shot fresh orange juice

1 shot fresh lemon juice

6 ice cubes

METHOD

1. Mix the salt and sugar on a saucer. Moisten the rim of a coupe glass with the lemon wedge, then dip it in the salt and sugar mix to coat.

2. Put the rest of the ingredients in a cocktail shaker and shake vigorously for 1 minute.

3. Strain into the glass and serve immediately.

Orange iced tea

SERVES: 4 | PREP TIME: 20 MINUTES

INGREDIENTS

2 Earl Grey tea bags

50 g / 1 ¾ oz / ½ cup sugar

50 ml / 1 ¾ fl. oz / ¼ cup orange liqueur

ice

50 ml / 1 ¾ fl. oz / ¼ cup gin

1 orange, cut into wedges

mint leaves to garnish

METHOD

1. Place the tea bags into a jug and pour over 500 ml of boiling water.

2. Stir through the sugar and leave to steep for 15 minutes.

3. Add the orange liqueur, ice and gin and stir to cool.

4. Fill glasses with more ice and orange wedges.

5. Strain the iced tea into the glasses and garnish with mint.

Singapore sling

SERVES: 1 | PREP TIME: 5 MINUTES

INGREDIENTS

5 ice cubes

2 shots of pineapple juice

½ shot of herbal liqueur

½ shot of grenadine

½ shot of orange liqueur

1 shot of gin

1 shot of cherry brandy

soda water

TO SERVE:

a handful of redcurrants (optional)

METHOD

1. Put the ice cubes into a cocktail shaker.

2. Add the pineapple juice, herbal liqueur, grenadine, orange liqueur, gin and cherry brandy over the ice in the shaker, then shake for 20 seconds.

3. Pour into a tall glass and top up with soda water.

4. Serve sprinkled with redcurrants, if desired.

Whisky a go go

SERVES: 1 | PREP TIME: 5 MINUTES

INGREDIENTS

25 ml / 1 fl. oz bourbon

25 ml / 1 fl. oz orange liqueur

1 slice of lemon

METHOD

1. Combine the bourbon and orange liqueur in a shot glass.

2. Carefully place the lemon slice into the liquid.

3. Serve as a shot.

4. Drink the shot and then suck the lemon.

Pineapple mojito

SERVES: 1 | PREP TIME: 5 MINUTES

INGREDIENTS

4 fresh mint leaves, torn

1 lime, cut into wedges

2 shots golden rum

1 shot fresh lime juice

crushed ice

pineapple juice

TO SERVE:

1 wedge fresh pineapple

sprig of mint

METHOD

1. Put the torn mint and lime wedges in a highball glass and muddle to release the juice.

2. Add the rum and lime and stir well, then fill the glass with crushed ice.

3. Top up with pineapple juice and stir.

4. Serve garnished with the wedge of pineapple and mint.

Boozy hot chocolate

SERVES: 1 | PREP TIME: 10 MINUTES

INGREDIENTS

50 ml / 1 ¾ fl. oz / ¼ cup double (heavy) cream

1 tsp chocolate spread

150 ml / 5 ¼ fl. oz / ⅔ cup whole milk

25 g / 1 oz / ¼ cup dark chocolate, chopped

35 ml / 1 ¼ fl. oz rum

cookie, to garnish

METHOD

1. Whip the cream until thick and smooth. Stir the chocolate spread through the whipped cream.

2. Heat the milk in a saucepan until simmering. Take off the heat and mix through the chocolate until it melts.

3. Return the chocolate to the hob and heat until warm, then stir through the rum.

4. Pour into a serving glass and top with the whipped cream and a broken cookie to garnish.

Iced Irish latte

SERVES: 1 | PREP TIME: 10 MINUTES

INGREDIENTS

1 single espresso

35 ml / 1 ¼ fl. oz Irish whisky

250 ml / 9 fl. oz / 1 cup milk

ice

METHOD

1. Make an espresso and set aside to cool for a few minutes.

2. Add the espresso, whisky, milk and ice into the cup of a blender.

3. Blender for 30 seconds until smooth.

4. Pour into a glass and serve.

Blueberry G&T

SERVES: 1 | PREP TIME: 5 MINUTES

INGREDIENTS

a handful of fresh blueberries

50 ml / 1 ¾ fl. oz / ¼ cup gin

ice

200 ml / 7 fl. oz / ¾ cup tonic water

METHOD

1. Place half the blueberries into a glass and the other half into a cocktail shaker.

2. Pour the gin into the shaker with the berries and add a scoop of ice.

3. Shake together for 30 seconds.

4. Strain the gin into the glass and top up with tonic water.

Raspberry beret

SERVES: 1 | PREP TIME: 5 MINUTES

INGREDIENTS

50 g / 1 ¾ oz / ½ cup fresh raspberries

50 ml / 1 ¾ fl. oz / ¼ cup vodka

1 lemon, juiced

ice

soda water

mint leaves and raspberries to garnish

METHOD

1. Place the fresh raspberries, vodka and lemon juice in a cocktail shaker half filled with ice.

2. Shake vigorously for 30 seconds.

3. Strain into glasses half filled with ice.

4. Top up with soda water and garnish with mint and fresh raspberries.

Casablanca

SERVES: 1 | PREP TIME: 5 MINUTES

INGREDIENTS

6 ice cubes

2 shots of white rum

½ shot of cherry liqueur

1 shot of triple sec

1 shot of lemon juice

1 orange, cut into wedges

TO SERVE:

1 lemon wedge

METHOD

1. Put the ice into a cocktail shaker.

2. Pour the white rum, cherry liqueur, triple sec and lemon juice over the ice in the cocktail shaker, then shake for 20 seconds.

3. Pour into a glass and squeeze the juice from the orange wedges into the cocktail.

4. Serve immediately, garnished with a lemon wedge.

Classic lime daiquiri

SERVES: 1 | PREP TIME: 5-10 MINUTES

....

INGREDIENTS

50ml/2fl oz white rum

35ml/1½fl oz fresh lime juice

4 tsp sugar syrup

1 wedge lime

METHOD

1. Place the rum, lime juice and sugar syrup into a cocktail shaker and shake well to combine.

2. Pour into a martini glass and serve garnished with a wedge of lime.

Mojito royale

SERVES: 2 | PREP TIME: 5 MINUTES

INGREDIENTS

6 fresh mint leaves, torn, plus extra
sprigs to garnish

1 lime, sliced

4 shots white rum

1 ½ shots fresh lime juice

1 shot sugar syrup

crushed ice

Champagne, to top up

METHOD

1. Put the mint in a cocktail shaker with half of the sliced lime.

2. Add the rum, lime juice, sugar syrup and a scoop of crushed ice and shake vigorously for 30 seconds.

3. Divide between two Collins glasses and add more crushed ice to fill.

4. Top up with Champagne and garnish with extra mint sprigs and the rest of the sliced lime.

Cosmopoligin

SERVES: 1 | PREP TIME: 5 MINUTES

INGREDIENTS

2 shots London dry gin

2 shots triple sec

3 shots cranberry juice

1 shot fresh lime juice

6 ice cubes

METHOD

1. Put all of the ingredients in a cocktail shaker and shake vigorously for 1 minute.

2. Strain into two martini glasses and serve immediately.

Cucumber, lime and thyme cooler

MAKES: 1 LITRE | PREP TIME: 10 MINUTES

INGREDIENTS

1 cucumber

ice cubes

1 lime, sliced

1 small bunch fresh thyme

250 ml / 9 fl. oz / 1 cup vodka

250 ml / 9 fl. oz / 1 cup fresh lime juice

100 ml / 3 ½ fl. oz / ½ cup sugar syrup

mineral water

METHOD

1. Peel two-thirds of the cucumber, then process it through a juicer.

2. Use the vegetable peeler to slice the rest of the cucumber into very thin ribbons.

3. Half fill a large jug with ice cubes and add the cucumber ribbons, lime and thyme.

4. Add the rest of the cucumber juice, the vodka, lime juice and sugar syrup and stir for 1 minute.

5. Top up the jug with mineral water and serve immediately.

Berry shake

SERVES: 1 | PREP TIME: 5 MINUTES

INGREDIENTS

crushed ice

a handful of frozen raspberries

a handful of frozen strawberries

a handful of blueberries

4 shots semi-skimmed milk

2 shots orange juice, chilled

1 shot vodka

1 shot lime juice

TO SERVE:

2 frozen raspberries

2 blueberries

METHOD

1. Put all the ingredients in a blender and whizz for at least 30 seconds or until completely blended and smooth.

2. Pour the blended mixture into a glass.

3. Serve garnished with a couple of raspberries and blueberries.

Sex on the beach

SERVES: 1 | PREP TIME: 5 MINUTES

••••••••••••••••••••••••••

INGREDIENTS

a handful of ice cubes

2 shots vodka

1 shot peach schnapps

3 shots orange juice

3 shots cranberry juice

TO SERVE:

2 raspberries

sprig of mint

METHOD

1. Put ice into the shaker.

2. Add the vodka and peach schnapps over the ice in the shaker, then shake for 10 seconds.

3. Pour into a glass and top up with orange and cranberry juice.

4. Serve immediately with the raspberries and a sprig of mint.

Purple rain

SERVES: 1 | PREP TIME: 5 MINUTES

INGREDIENTS

2 handfuls blueberries

4 handfuls crushed ice

½ shot vodka

½ shot light rum

½ shot gin

½ shot bourbon whisky

½ shot blue Curaçao

lemonade

METHOD

1. Put the blueberries and 2 handfuls of crushed ice in a blender and whizz for 20 seconds.

2. Put the remaining 2 handfuls of crushed ice into the cocktail shaker.

3. Pour the vodka, light rum, gin, bourbon whisky and blue Curaçao over the crushed ice in the cocktail shaker, then shake for 20 seconds.

4. Pour into a glass and add the blended blueberries.

5. Stir well and serve immediately.

Cranberry Collins

SERVES: 2 | PREP TIME: 5 MINUTES

INGREDIENTS

a handful of fresh cranberries,
plus extra to garnish

2 sprigs fresh rosemary, plus extra to garnish

4 shots London dry gin

2 shots fresh lemon juice

3 shots sugar syrup

8 ice cubes

crushed ice, to serve

soda water

METHOD

1. Muddle the cranberries and rosemary in the base of a cocktail shaker to release the juice.

2. Add the gin, lemon juice, sugar syrup and ice cubes. Shake vigorously for 1 minute.

3. Fill two Collins glasses with crushed ice and strain the cocktail over the top.

4. Top up with soda water and garnish with rosemary sprigs and fresh cranberries.

Mint shake

SERVES: 1 | PREP TIME: 5-8 MINUTES

INGREDIENTS

1 ½ shots dark crème de cacao

1 shot white crème de menthe

1 shot Irish cream liqueur

1 tbsp unsweetened cocoa powder

1 scoop dark chocolate ice cream

1 scoop mint chocolate ice cream

4 ice cubes

TO SERVE:

whipped cream - 1 tbsp mint chocolate sauce

METHOD

1. Pour the crème de cacao, crème de menthe and Irish cream liqueur into a liquidizer.

2. Add the cocoa, ice cream and ice cubes and blend for 30 seconds or until completely smooth.

3. Pour the cocktail into a glass, garnish with plenty of whipped cream and pour over some mint chocolate sauce.

Boozy berry smoothie

SERVES: 2 | PREP TIME: 15 MINUTES

INGREDIENTS

1 banana, sliced

150 g / 5 ¼ oz frozen mixed berries

250 ml / 9 fl. oz / 1 cup milk

250 g / 9 oz / 1 cup low-fat yogurt

35 ml / 1 ¼ fl. oz vodka

25 ml / 1 fl. oz crème de cassis

METHOD

1. Place the ingredients into a blender, reserving some of the berries for the top.

2. Blend on high for 30 seconds to 1 minute until smooth.

3. Pour into glasses.

4. Top with the reserved berries.

Fruity gin fizz

SERVES: 1 | PREP TIME: 5 MINUTES

INGREDIENTS

2 shots London dry gin

1 shot fresh lemon juice

½ shot sugar syrup

12 ice cubes

1 strawberry, sliced

2 slices orange, halved

½ tsp fresh thyme leaves

soda water

METHOD

1. Put the gin, lemon juice and sugar syrup in a cocktail shaker with half of the ice cubes. Shake vigorously for 1 minute.

2. Put the strawberry, orange and thyme in a mason jar glass, then add the rest of the ice.

3. Strain the cocktail into the glass and top up with soda water.

Rosemary and elderflower Collins

SERVES: 1 | PREP TIME: 10 MINUTES

INGREDIENTS

1 lemon

2 sprigs fresh rosemary, plus extra to garnish

2 shots London dry gin

1 shot fresh lemon juice

1 ½ shots elderflower cordial

8 ice cubes

ice cubes, to serve

soda water

METHOD

1. Use a vegetable peeler to shave a long ribbon of lemon zest and reserve, then cut the rest of the lemon into cubes. Muddle the cubed lemon with the rosemary in the base of a cocktail shaker.

2. Add the gin, lemon juice, elderflower cordial and ice cubes.

3. Shake vigorously for 1 minute.

4. Fill a Collins glass with ice cubes and strain the cocktail over the top.

5. Top up with soda water, then wrap the reserved ribbon of lemon zest around a rosemary sprig and use to garnish the drink.

Kiwi and blueberry mojito

SERVES: 1 | PREP TIME: 10 MINUTES

INGREDIENTS

1 tsp caster (superfine) sugar

a handful of fresh mint

½ kiwi, sliced

a handful of blueberries

50 ml / 1 ¾ fl. oz / ¼ cup white rum

soda water

METHOD

1. Place the sugar and mint into a tall glass and muddle together.

2. Add the kiwi, blueberries and rum.

3. Top up the glass with soda water and stir.

Blue Monday

SERVES: 1 | PREP TIME: 5 MINUTES

INGREDIENTS

ice

35 ml / 1 ¼ fl. oz vodka

25 ml / 1 fl. oz blue curaçao

1 lime, juiced

lemonade

mint to garnish

METHOD

1. Three quarters fill a highball glass with ice.

2. Pour the vodka, curaçao and lime juice into the glass.

3. Top up with lemonade.

4. Garnish with mint.

Cucumber and mint cooler

SERVES: 2 | PREP TIME: 10 MINUTES

INGREDIENTS

35 ml / 1 ¼ fl. oz gin

35 ml / 1 ¼ fl. oz vodka

1 lime, juiced

1 tsp caster (superfine) sugar

a handful of mint leaves

6 slices of cucumber

ice

tonic water

METHOD

1. Half fill a cocktail shaker with ice.

2. Add the gin, vodka, lime juice, sugar and half the mint leaves into the shaker and shake for 30 seconds.

3. Add the remaining mint, cucumber and ice to lowball glasses.

4. Strain the cocktail shaker into the glasses.

5. Top up with tonic water

Cran jam

SERVES: 4 | PREP TIME: 5 MINUTES

INGREDIENTS

100 ml / 3 ½ fl. oz / ½ cup vodka

100 ml / 3 ½ fl. oz / ½ cup cranberry juice

ice

METHOD

1. Place the vodka and cranberry juice into a shaker half filled with ice.

2. Shake vigorously for 30 seconds.

3. Strain the cocktail into shot glasses to serve.

Green heaven

SERVES: 2 | PREP TIME: 5 MINUTES

INGREDIENTS

4 sprigs mint

4 shots sake

2 shots vodka

2 shots triple sec

2 shots fresh lime juice

1 shot sugar syrup

100 ml / 3 ½ fl. oz / ½ cup chilled mineral water

2 tsp matcha green tea powder

2 handfuls ice cubes

½ lime, sliced

METHOD

1. Muddle half of the mint in the base of a cocktail shaker. Add the sake, vodka, triple sec, lime juice, sugar syrup, water and matcha.

2. Add a handful of ice cubes and shake vigorously for 1 minute.

3. Divide the rest of the ice between two glasses and add the sliced lime and remaining mint sprigs. Strain over the cocktail and serve immediately.

Fuschia lemonade

SERVES: 1 LITRE | PREP TIME: 5 MINUTES

INGREDIENTS

ice cubes

3 shots raspberry liqueur

2 shots blue Curaçao

150 ml / 5 ½ fl. oz / ⅔ cup fresh lemon juice

3 shots sugar syrup

1 lemon, sliced

75 g / 2 ½ oz / ½ cup strawberries, quartered

soda water

METHOD

1. Half fill a large jug with ice cubes. Add the rest of the ingredients, apart from the soda water, and stir for 1 minute.

2. Top up the jug with soda water, then pour into glasses.

3. Garnish with mint sprigs and serve immediately.

Green tea mojito

SERVES: 1 | PREP TIME: 5 MINUTES

• •

INGREDIENTS

1 tsp green tea

ice

a handful of mint leaves

1 tsp caster (superfine) sugar

1 lime, cut into wedges

50 ml / 1 ¾ fl. oz / ¼ cup rum

METHOD

1. Brew the green tea in 150 ml water and place ice into the glass to cool.

2. Place the mint leaves, sugar and lime into the bottom of a tall glass.

3. Muddle the lime, sugar, and mint together until the sugar has dissolved and the mint leaves are bruised.

4. Add the rum and top the glass up with ice.

5. Strain the cold green tea into the glass.

113

Hot apple toddy

SERVES: 5 | PREP TIME: 5 MINUTES | COOKING TIME: 5 MINUTES

INGREDIENTS

250 ml / 9 fl. oz / 1 cup apple juice

2 cinnamon sticks, halved

2 star anise

4 cloves

6 brown sugar cubes

4 shots whisky

½ eating apple, sliced

METHOD

1. Put the apple juice in a small saucepan with the cinnamon, star anise, cloves and sugar cubes.

2. Stir over a low heat to dissolve the sugar, then bring to a simmer.

3. Measure the whisky into two glass mugs and add the sliced apple.

4. Divide the mulled apple juice and spices between the cups.

5. Serve immediately.

Summer garita

SERVES: 1 | PREP TIME: 5 MINUTES

INGREDIENTS

3 ice cubes

1 shot lime juice

1 shot elderflower cordial

2 shots pineapple juice

pink lemonade

TO SERVE:

2 strawberries, quartered

2 ice cubes

METHOD

1. Put the ice cubes into a cocktail shaker.

2. Pour the lime juice, elderflower cordial and pineapple juice over the ice cubes in the cocktail shaker, then shake for 10 seconds.

3. Strain the mixture into a margarita glass, topping it up with pink lemonade.

4. Serve with some strawberry quarters and extra ice cubes.

Greena-colada

SERVES: 1 | PREP TIME: 5 MINUTES

INGREDIENTS

2 handfuls spinach leaves, washed

a handful of kiwi chunks

3 ice cubes

2 shots white rum

2 shots coconut cream

pineapple juice

TO SERVE:

sprig of mint

METHOD

1. Put the spinach leaves and kiwi chunks in a blender and whizz for 30 seconds.

2. Put the ice cubes into a cocktail shaker.

3. Strain the blended fruit into the cocktail shaker then add the white rum and coconut cream over the ice in the shaker and shake for at least 30 seconds.

4. Pour into a glass and top up with pineapple juice. Stir well with a cocktail mixer.

5. Serve garnished with a sprig of mint.

Ultimate rum hot chocolate

SERVES: 1 | PREP TIME: 5-8 MINUTES

INGREDIENTS

2 shots coconut rum

hot chocolate, made with milk

TO SERVE:

whipped cream

2 tsp chocolate shavings (optional)

2 walnuts (optional)

deluxe chocolates (optional)

METHOD

1. Pour the coconut rum into a thick, heat-proof glass.

2. Add the hot chocolate and stir well, ensuring the hot chocolate is fully warmed.

3. Top with whipped cream and chocolate shavings, walnuts and chocolates, if desired.

4. Serve immediately.

Strawberry dream

SERVES: 1 | PREP TIME: 5 MINUTES

INGREDIENTS

150 g / 5 ¼ oz / 1 cup fresh strawberries,
plus extra to garnish

100 g / 3 ½ oz yogurt ice cream

200 ml / 7 fl. oz / ¾ cup almond milk

35 ml / 1 ¼ fl. oz almond liqueur or amaretto

METHOD

1. Hull and halve the strawberries.

2. Place the ingredients into the cup of a
blender and blend for 1 minute until thick
and combined.

3. Pour into a glass and garnish with additional
strawberries and a sprig of mint, if desired.

Irish buck

SERVES: 1 | PREP TIME: 5 MINUTES

INGREDIENTS

ice

50 ml / 1 ¾ fl. oz / ¼ cup Irish whisky

200 ml / 7 fl. oz / ¾ cup ginger ale

1 lime wedge

METHOD

1. Half fill a lowball glass with ice cubes.

2. Pour over the whisky.

3. Top up with the ginger ale.

4. Squeeze the lime juice into the glass and stir.

Smooth peach punch

SERVES: 1 | PREP TIME: 10 MINUTES

●●●●●●●●●●●●●●●●●●●●●●●●●●●●

INGREDIENTS

2 fresh peaches

50 g / 1 ¾ oz / ½ cup pineapple chunks

1 banana, sliced

100 ml / 3 ½ fl. oz / ½ cup peach juice

1 lemon, juiced

35 ml / 1 ¼ fl. oz peach schnapps

25 ml / 1 fl. oz amaretto

ice

METHOD

1. Halve and destone the peaches before adding to a blender.

2. Add the pineapple chunks and banana before blending on high for 1 minute until thick.

3. Add the peach juice, lemon and alcohol and blend quickly again.

4. Pour into chilled serving glasses with some ice in the bottom.

Mint ginfusion

SERVES: 1 | PREP TIME: 5 MINUTES

INGREDIENTS

2 handfuls ice cubes

2 shots lime juice

½ shot lime cordial

½ tsp sugar syrup

1 tsp mint syrup

5 mint leaves

2 shots gin

soda water

TO SERVE:

a handful of blueberries

sprig of mint

METHOD

1. Put the ice into a cocktail shaker.

2. Put the lime juice, lime cordial, sugar syrup, mint syrup, mint leaves and gin in the cocktail shaker, then shake for 20 seconds, aiming to crush the mint leaves to release flavour.

3. Strain the mixture into a glass, topping it up with soda water.

4. Serve garnished with a handful of blueberries and sprig of mint.

5. If desired, thread some blueberries onto a cocktail stick and rest it in the glass for added decoration.

Clumsy gardener

SERVES: 1 | PREP TIME: 5 MINUTES

INGREDIENTS

5 ice cubes

sprig of mint

2 shots gin

2 shots pineapple juice

1 shot lemon juice

½ shot of grenadine

TO SERVE:

1 large pineapple wedge

METHOD

1. Put the ice cubes into a cocktail shaker.

2. Add the mint, gin, pineapple juice, lemon juice and grenadine to the cocktail shaker, then shake for 30 seconds.

3. Pour into a glass or jar.

4. Serve garnished with a large wedge of pineapple.

PS I love you

SERVES: 1 | PREP TIME: 5 MINUTES

INGREDIENTS

3 ice cubes

½ shot dark rum

½ shot amaretto

1 shot Irish cream liqueur

½ shot coffee liqueur

2 shots cream

3 shots milk

METHOD

1. Put the ice cubes into a cocktail shaker.

2. Pour the dark rum, amaretto, Irish cream liqueur, coffee liqueur, cream and milk over the ice in the cocktail shaker, then shake for 20 seconds.

3. Strain into a glass and serve immediately.

Fruity Manhattan

SERVES: 1 | PREP TIME: 5 MINUTES

INGREDIENTS

5 ice cubes

1 shot bourbon whisky

1 shot sweet red vermouth

1 dash bitters

a handful of strawberries,
chopped into large chunks

METHOD

1. Put the ice into a cocktail shaker.

2. Add the bourbon whisky, sweet red
vermouth and bitters.

3. Strain into a glass and add the strawberries.

4. Serve immediately, garnished with mint
sprigs if desired.

Lychee martini

SERVES: 1 | PREP TIME: 5 MINUTES

INGREDIENTS

2 shots vodka

2 shots lychee juice

2 shots pink grapefruit juice, chilled

8 ice cubes

TO SERVE:

½ fresh lychee

METHOD

1. Put the vodka, lychee juice and grapefruit juice in a cocktail shaker.

2. Add the ice to the shaker and shake vigorously for 1 minute.

3. Strain into a coupe glass and serve immediately, garnished with half a lychee.

Strawberry and blood orange punch

MAKES: 750ML | PREP TIME: 5 MINUTES

INGREDIENTS

10 ripe strawberries

250 ml / 9 fl. oz / 1 cup blood orange juice, chilled

175 ml / 6 fl. oz / ⅔ cup London dry gin

100 ml / 3 ½ fl. oz / ½ cup red vermouth

2 limes, juiced

100 ml / 3 ½ fl. oz / ½ cup sugar syrup

2 egg whites

ice cubes

METHOD

1. Put all of the ingredients, except the ice, in a liquidizer and blend until smooth and frothy.

2. Pour the punch into an ice-filled jug and stir well to chill.

3. Serve immediately.

Pink martini

SERVES: 1 | PREP TIME: 5 MINUTES

INGREDIENTS

2 shots London dry gin

½ shot sweet white vermouth

2 shots pink grapefruit juice

1 shot cranberry juice

6 ice cubes

TO SERVE:

1 curl lime zest

METHOD

1. Put the gin, vermouth, grapefruit juice and cranberry juice in a mixing glass with the ice cubes.

2. Stir briskly for 30 seconds, then strain the cocktail into a martini glass.

3. Garnish with a curl of lime zest and serve immediately.

Peach sangria

SERVES: 4-6 | PREP TIME: 10 MINUTES

INGREDIENTS

750 ml / 25 ⅓ fl. oz / 3 cups red wine

50 ml / 1 ¾ fl. oz / ¼ cup orange liqueur

100 ml / 3 ½ fl. oz / ½ cup peach schnapps

2 tbsp caster (superfine) sugar

2 lemons, sliced

a handful of mint leaves

ice

500 ml / 17 fl. oz / 2 cups soda water

METHOD

1. Pour the wine, orange liqueur, peach schnapps and sugar into a bowl and mix until the sugar dissolves.

2. Add the lemons, mint leaves and ice and stir to chill. Place into the refrigerator until required.

3. Pour into glasses half filled with ice and top up with soda water.

Bramble julep

SERVES: 1 | PREP TIME: 5 MINUTES

INGREDIENTS

2 sprigs mint

1 slice lemon, halved

1 shot raspberry eau de vie

1 shot blackberry eau de vie

1 shot sugar syrup

8 ice cubes

a handful of fresh raspberries

chilled mineral water

3 blackberries

METHOD

1. Put the mint, lemon, eau de vies, sugar syrup and ice in a cocktail shaker and shake vigorously for 1 minute.

2. Put the raspberries in a rocks glass and pour in the cocktail without straining.

3. Top up with chilled mineral water.

4. Garnish with the blackberries and serve immediately.

Raspberry smoothie shooter

SERVES: 4 | PREP TIME: 10 MINUTES

INGREDIENTS

50 g / 1 ¾ oz / ½ cup raspberries

crushed ice

150 ml / 5 ¼ fl. oz / ⅔ cup raspberry vodka

½ lemon juice

mint leaves

METHOD

1. Place the raspberries into a blender, reserving some for garnish, and blend to a purée.

2. Sieve the juice into a bowl and clean the blender.

3. Add the raspberry juice, ice, vodka and lemon juice back into the blender and quickly blend together until smooth.

4. Pour into tall shooter glasses and top with the reserved berries and mint leaves.

Pimm's cup

SERVES: 1 | PREP TIME: 5 MINUTES

INGREDIENTS

2 shots Pimm's No.1 cup

4 slices cucumber

3 orange wedges

6 ice cubes

lemonade

METHOD

1. Measure the Pimm's into a highball glass.

2. Add the cucumber, orange and ice to the glass, then stir gently to mix.

3. Top up with lemonade.

4. Serve immediately.

Mint lemon drop

SERVES: 1 | PREP TIME: 5 MINUTES

INGREDIENTS

crushed ice

2 shots vodka

2 shots lemon juice

1 shot lime juice

1 mint sprig

1 tsp sugar syrup

lemonade

1 lemon wedge

1 lime wedge

TO SERVE:

1 lime slice

METHOD

1. Put the crushed ice into a cocktail shaker.

2. Add the vodka, lemon juice and lime juice over the ice in the shaker, then shake for 10 seconds.

3. Crush the mint sprig and add it with the sugar syrup to the glass, then pour in the mixture from the shaker.

4. Top up with lemonade.

5. Run the extra lemon wedge and lime wedge around the edge of the glass for added flavour.

6. Serve immediately, garnished with a lime slice.

Pink flamingo

SERVES: 1 | PREP TIME: 5 MINUTES

INGREDIENTS

crushed ice

2 shots white rum

1 shot grenadine

1 shot lime juice

2 shots pineapple juice

TO SERVE:

sprig of mint

METHOD

1. Put the crushed ice into a cocktail shaker.

2. Pour the white rum, grenadine, lime juice and pineapple juice over the crushed ice in the cocktail shaker, then shake for 10 seconds.

3. Pour into a tall glass and serve immediately, garnished with mint or a lime slice.

Perky cactus

SERVES: 1 | PREP TIME: 5 MINUTES

INGREDIENTS

3 ice cubes

1 shot tequila

½ shot blue Curaçao

1 shot orange juice, strained

1 shot pineapple juice

1 shot lemon juice

½ shot peach juice

TO SERVE:

extra ice cubes

1 peach wedge

METHOD

1. Put the ice into a cocktail shaker.

2. Pour the tequila, blue Curaçao, orange juice, pineapple juice, lemon juice and peach juice over the ice in the cocktail shaker, then shake for 30 seconds.

3. Strain into a glass and top with extra ice and a wedge of peach.

Citron zorbet

SERVES: 1 | PREP TIME: 5 MINUTES

INGREDIENTS

2 handfuls ice cubes

1 shot lemon liqueur

1 shot vodka

1 shot lemon juice

1 tsp sugar syrup

METHOD

1. Put the ice cubes into a cocktail shaker.

2. Add the lemon liqueur, vodka, lemon juice and sugar syrup, then shake for 20 seconds.

3. Strain into a glass and serve immediately.

Salty orange fizz

SERVES: 1 | PREP TIME: 10 MINUTES

INGREDIENTS

salt

ice

½ orange

35 ml / 1 ¼ fl. oz gin

1 tbsp lemon juice

2 tsp orange liqueur

1 tsp simple syrup

2 drops of bitters

soda water

orange wedge and rosemary sprigs to garnish

METHOD

1. Wet the rim of a lowball glass and dip into the salt.

2. Half fill the glass with ice to chill.

3. Juice the orange and set aside.

4. Add the gin, lemon, liqueur, syrup and bitters to a cocktail shaker and half fill with ice.

5. Shake well and strain into the prepared glass.

6. Top up with the orange juice and then soda water.

7. Garnish with an orange wedge and rosemary sprig.

Iced tea punch

SERVES: 2 | PREP TIME: 10 MINUTES | CHILLING TIME: 30 MINUTES

INGREDIENTS

2 Earl Grey tea bags

1 tbsp caster (superfine) sugar

50 ml / 1 ¾ fl. oz / ¼ cup vermouth rosso

50 ml / 1 ¾ fl. oz / ¼ cup vodka

2 lemons, sliced

ice

a handful of mint leaves

METHOD

1. Place the tea bags into a jug of boiling water containing roughly 300ml.

2. Leave to steep for 5 minutes, remove the tea bags and then stir in the sugar.

3. Place into the refrigerator to chill for 30 minutes

4. Stir the vermouth and vodka into the tea and add the lemons, ice and mint.

5. Pour into serving glasses and garnish with wedges of lemon.

Magnificent Rita

SERVES: 1 | PREP TIME: 10 MINUTES | FREEZING TIME: 4 HOURS

INGREDIENTS

100 g / 3 ½ oz honeydew melon

30 ml / 1 fl. oz tequila

1 lime juiced

a handful of mint leaves

15 ml / ½ fl. oz melon liqueur

ice

METHOD

1. Place the melon into the freezer for 4 hours or until frozen.

2. Place the melon into a blender with the tequila, lime, mint leaves, liqueur and a handful of ice.

3. Blend for 1 minute or until smooth.

4. Pour into a glass and garnish with mint leaves.

149

Strawberry mojito

SERVES: 2 | PREP TIME: 5 MINUTES

INGREDIENTS

2 sprigs spearmint, plus extra to garnish

1 lime, cut into wedges

6 strawberries, quartered

4 shots white rum

2 shots fresh lime juice

ice cubes

soda water

METHOD

1. Put the mint, lime wedges and strawberries in two highball glasses and muddle to release the juice.

2. Add the rum and lime and stir well, then fill the glass with ice cubes.

3. Top up with soda and stir, then serve garnished with the extra mint.

Pomegranate punch

SERVES: 1 | PREP TIME: 5 MINUTES

INGREDIENTS

4 ice cubes

1 tsp sugar syrup

1 shot lime juice

6 shots pomegranate juice

1 tbsp pomegranate seeds

lemonade

TO SERVE:

1 tbsp pomegranate seeds

sprig of mint

METHOD

1. Put the ice cubes into a cocktail shaker.

2. Pour the sugar syrup, lime juice, pomegranate juice and seeds over the ice cubes in the cocktail shaker, then shake for 20 seconds.

3. Pour into a glass and top up with lemonade.

4. Serve garnished with more pomegranate seeds and a sprig of mint.

152

Summer field

SERVES: 1 | PREP TIME: 5 MINUTES

INGREDIENTS

2 kiwis, peeled

1 shot gin

1 shot advocaat

2 shots orange juice

2 shots passion fruit juice (or tropical juice)

METHOD

1. Put the kiwis in a blender and whizz for at least 30 seconds or until completely blended and smooth.

2. Meanwhile, pour the gin, advocaat, orange juice and passion fruit juice into a glass or jar.

3. Add the blended kiwi to the cocktail mixture then stir thoroughly.

4. Serve immediately with crushed ice, if desired.

153

Raspberry refresher

SERVES: 2 | PREP TIME: 10 MINUTES

INGREDIENTS

70 ml / 2 ⅓ fl. oz / ⅓ cup raspberry vodka

ice

2 slices of lemon

a handful of fresh raspberries

300 ml / 10 ½ fl. oz / 1 ¼ cups lemonade

mint leaves to garnish

METHOD

1. Divide the vodka between two glasses.

2. Add ice, lemon and fresh raspberries.

3. Top up with the lemonade and stir.

4. Garnish with mint.

Lemon crush

SERVES: 1 | PREP TIME: 5 MINUTES

INGREDIENTS

1 tbsp caster (superfine) sugar

2 lemons, juiced

50 ml / 1 ¾ fl. oz / ¼ cup gin

2 drops of bitters

crushed ice

mint leaves

METHOD

1. Add the sugar, lemon juice, gin and bitters into the cup of a blender.

2. Add a cup full of crushed ice and blend for 30 seconds until combined.

3. Pour into a serving glass.

4. Garnish with mint leaves.

Orange strawberry fizz

SERVES: 1 | PREP TIME: 5 MINUTES

INGREDIENTS

50 g / 1 ¾ oz / ½ cup strawberries

½ orange, sliced

35 ml / 1 ¼ fl. oz vodka

ice

soda water

METHOD

1. Wash the strawberries, dehull and slice in half.

2. Place the strawberries and orange into a cocktail shaker and gently muddle to release some juice.

3. Pour the vodka into the shaker and half fill with ice.

4. Shake briefly to combine before pouring into a glass.

5. Top up with the soda water.

Strawberry gin smash

SERVES: 1 | PREP TIME: 10 MINUTES

INGREDIENTS

½ tsp sugar

1 lime wedge

50 ml / 1 ¾ fl. oz / ¼ cup gin

2 slices of lemon

4 strawberries, halved

ice

soda water

mint leaves to garnish

METHOD

1. Place the sugar into a tall glass and add the lime wedge. Muddle together to dissolve the sugar.

2. Add the gin, lemon and strawberries.

3. Top the glass up with ice.

4. Fill the glass with soda water and stir to combine.

5. Garnish with mint.

Green monster

SERVES: 1 | PREP TIME: 10 MINUTES

INGREDIENTS

50 g / 1 ¾ oz / ½ cup spinach

250 ml / 9 fl. oz / 1 cup apple juice

40 ml / 1 ⅓ fl. oz vodka

crushed ice

METHOD

1. Wash the spinach to remove any dirt and grit.

2. Place the spinach and apple juice into a blender and blend until smooth

3. Half fill a glass with crushed ice and pour over the vodka.

4. Top up with the spinach and apple juice.

Mint gin ricky

SERVES: 1 | PREP TIME: 5 MINUTES

INGREDIENTS

ice

50 ml / 1 ¾ fl. oz / ¼ cup gin

½ lime, sliced

5-6 mint leaves

soda water

METHOD

1. Add the ice to a lowball glass.

2. Pour over the gin.

3. Add the lime and mint to the glass.

4. Top up with soda water and stir to mix.

Mulled cider

SERVES: 4-6 | PREP TIME: 10 MINUTES | COOKING TIME: 30 MINUTES

INGREDIENTS

1 l / 33 ¾ fl. oz / 4 cups dry cider

50 ml / 1 ¾ fl. oz / ¼ cup calvados

500 ml / 17 fl. oz / 2 cups apple juice

75 g / 2 ½ oz / ½ cup soft brown sugar

2 clementines, zest and segments

4 cloves

2 cinnamon sticks

1 lemon, sliced

METHOD

1. Place the cider, calvados, apple juice and sugar into a saucepan.

2. Heat until simmering and stir so that the sugar has dissolved.

3. Add the clementine zest and segments, cloves, cinnamon and lemon slices. Reduce the heat to a simmer and cover for 30 minutes.

4. Ladle into cups when ready.

Alabama slammer

SERVES: 1 | PREP TIME: 5 MINUTES

INGREDIENTS

4 ice cubes

½ shot bourbon whisky

½ shot amaretto

½ shot sloe gin

2 shots orange juice

TO SERVE:

1 orange wedge

METHOD

1. Put the ice into a cocktail shaker.

2. Pour the bourbon whisky, amaretto, sloe gin and orange juice over the ice in the cocktail shaker, then shake for 10 seconds.

3. Strain into a glass and serve immediately, garnished with an orange wedge.

Peach fizz

SERVES: 1 | PREP TIME: 5 MINUTES

●●●●●●●●●●●●●●●●●●●●●●●●

INGREDIENTS

35 ml / 1 ¼ fl. oz peach schnapps

100 ml / 3 ½ fl. oz / ½ cup peach juice

ice

125 ml / 4 ¼ fl. oz / ½ cup prosecco

1 sprig of rosemary and peach slices to garnish

METHOD

1. Pour the schnapps and peach juice over a glass with ice.

2. Stir for 20 seconds to combine and chill.

3. Top up the glass with the prosecco.

4. Garnish with rosemary and a peach wedge.

167

Kiwi and mint tea

SERVES: 1 | PREP TIME: 5 MINUTES

INGREDIENTS

½ kiwi, sliced

a handful of mint leaves

1 lime, juiced

25 ml / 1 fl. oz simple syrup

50 ml / 1 ¾ fl. oz / ¼ cup vodka

200 ml / 7 fl. oz / ¾ cup water

ice

METHOD

1. Half fill a lowball glass with ice.

2. Muddle the kiwi and mint in a cocktail shaker.

3. Fill the remaining half with ice and add the lime, syrup, vodka and water.

4. Shake vigorously for 30 seconds.

5. Strain in the prepared glass and garnish with kiwi and mint leaves.

Strawberry heaven

SERVES: 1 | PREP TIME: 5 MINUTES

INGREDIENTS

150 g / 5 ¼ oz strawberry ice cream

200 ml / 7 fl. oz / ¾ cup whole milk

50 ml / 1 ¾ fl. oz / ¼ cup vanilla vodka

whipped cream

METHOD

1. Place the ice cream, milk and vodka into a blender.

2. Blend for 1 minute until smooth.

3. Pour into a chilled glass.

4. Top with the whipped cream.

Pink paradise

SERVES: 1 | PREP TIME: 5 MINUTES

INGREDIENTS

ice

1 tsp pomegranate syrup

1 lime, juiced

50 ml / 1 ¾ fl. oz / ¼ cup raspberry vodka

250 ml / 9 fl. oz / 1 cup soda water

lime slices to garnish

METHOD

1. Half fill a highball glass with ice.

2. Place ice into the cup of a cocktail shaker.

3. Add the syrup, lime juice and vodka.

4. Replace the cup of the shaker and shake for 30 seconds to combine.

5. Strain the cocktail into the prepared glass and top up with soda water.

6. Garnish with slices of lime.

Blues-berry cooler

SERVES: 2 | PREP TIME: 10 MINUTES

INGREDIENTS

100 g / 3 ½ oz / ⅔ cup blueberries, fresh or frozen

1 tbsp sugar

1 lemon, juiced

100 ml / 3 ½ fl. oz / ½ cup gin

2 drops of bitters

100 ml / 3 ½ fl. oz / ½ cup blueberry juice

lemon and mint to garnish

METHOD

1. Place the blueberries, sugar and lemon into a glass and muddle together until the sugar has dissolved.

2. Strain into a cocktail shaker half filled with ice.

3. Add the gin and bitters and shake vigorously to combine for 30 seconds.

4. Strain into glasses half filled with ice and top up with blueberry juice.

5. Garnish with lemon and mint

Raspberry limoncello fizz

SERVES: 1 | PREP TIME: 5 MINUTES

INGREDIENTS

1 shot vodka

2 shots limoncello

1 shot fresh lemon juice

6 ice cubes

Prosecco, to top up

6 fresh raspberries

1 sprig mint

METHOD

1. Measure the vodka, limoncello and lemon juice into a cocktail shaker and add the ice.

2. Shake vigorously for 1 minute, then strain into a highball glass.

3. Top up with Prosecco and float the raspberries and mint on top.

Pineapple margarita

SERVES: 1 | PREP TIME: 5 MINUTES

INGREDIENTS

2 handfuls ice cubes

2 shots tequila

1 shot triple sec

3 shots pineapple juice

½ shot lime juice

lime wedge

1 tsp salt

METHOD

1. Put the ice cubes into the cocktail shaker.

2. Pour the tequila, triple sec, pineapple juice and lime juice over the ice cubes in the cocktail shaker, then shake for 20 seconds.

3. Rub the lime wedge around the rim of the glass, then dip in salt.

4. Pour the cocktail mixture into the martini glass and add more ice cubes, if desired.

Frozen mulberry daiquiri

SERVES: 1 | PREP TIME: 5 MINUTES | FREEZING TIME: 2 HOURS

INGREDIENTS

2 tbsp fresh mulberries

2 strawberries, quartered

½ banana, peeled and sliced

2 shots white rum

½ shot fresh lime juice

4 ice cubes

1 mint sprig, to garnish

METHOD

1. Spread out the mulberries, strawberries and banana on a baking tray and freeze for at least 2 hours. They can then be stored in a freezer bag for later use or used straight away.

2. Put the frozen fruit in a liquidizer with the rum, lime juice and ice. Blend until very smooth.

3. Pour the cocktail into a glass and serve garnished with mint.

Raspberry slammer

SERVES: 2 | PREP TIME: 5 MINUTES

INGREDIENTS

35 ml / 1 ¼ fl. oz raspberry vodka

35 ml / 1 ¼ fl. oz white tequila

a handful of fresh raspberries

lemonade

mint leaves

METHOD

1. Divide the vodka and tequila between two tall shooter glasses.

2. Add some fresh berries to the glasses.

3. Top up with lemonade.

4. Garnish with mint leaves.

Cranberry slam

SERVES: 4 | PREP TIME: 5 MINUTES

INGREDIENTS

100 ml / 3 ½ fl. oz / ½ cup cranberry vodka

ice

soda water

fresh cranberries (optional)

METHOD

1. Divide the vodka between 4 shot glasses.

2. Place an ice cube in each.

3. Top up with some soda water.

4. Garnish with fresh cranberries if desired.

Peach julep

SERVES: 1 | PREP TIME: 5 MINUTES

INGREDIENTS

¼ peach, sliced

1 lime, juiced

30 ml / 1 fl. oz simple syrup

30 ml / 1 fl. oz peach schnapps

30 ml / 1 fl. oz bourbon

200 ml / 7 fl. oz / ¾ cup water

ice

METHOD

1. Half fill a lowball glass with ice and the peach slices.

2. Pour the lime, syrup, schnapps and bourbon into a cocktail shaker half filled with ice.

3. Shake vigorously for 30 seconds.

4. Strain in the prepared glass and garnish with mint if desired.

181

Red wine punch

SERVES: 4-6 | PREP TIME: 30 MINUTES

INGREDIENTS

750 ml / 25 ⅓ fl. oz / 3 cups red wine

50 ml / 1 ¾ fl. oz / ¼ cup brandy

50 ml / 1 ¾ fl. oz / ¼ cup orange liqueur

1 lemon, sliced

2 cinnamon sticks

ice

METHOD

1. Pour the wine, brandy and orange liqueur into a jug.

2. Add the lemon and cinnamon and top up with ice.

3. Stir to combine and place into the refrigerator for at least 30 minutes.

4. Pour into glasses to serve, ensuring that some ice and lemon goes into each.

Cucumber and mint fizz

SERVES: 1 | PREP TIME: 5 MINUTES

INGREDIENTS

5 cm (2 in) cucumber, diced,
plus 1 slice to garnish

6 mint leaves

2 shots London dry gin

8 ice cubes

tonic water

METHOD

1. Muddle the cucumber and mint in the bottom of a cocktail shaker.

2. Add the gin and six ice cubes and shake vigorously for 1 minute.

3. Strain into a glass and add the remaining two ice cubes.

4. Top up with tonic water to taste.

5. Garnish with a cucumber slice and serve.

Strawberry serenade

SERVES: 1 | PREP TIME: 5 MINUTES

INGREDIENTS

a handful of mint leaves

½ lime, juiced

50 ml / 1 ¾ fl. oz / ¼ cup strawberry vodka

ice

lemonade

fresh strawberries to garnish

METHOD

1. Place the mint and lime juice into the base of a glass and muddle together.

2. Add the vodka and half fill the glass with ice.

3. Top up with lemonade and garnish with fresh strawberries.

Raspberry and mint julep

SERVES: 1 | PREP TIME: 5 MINUTES

INGREDIENTS

2 sprigs mint

2 shots raspberry eau de vie

1 shot sugar syrup

8 ice cubes

a handful of fresh raspberries

chilled mineral water

METHOD

1. Put the mint, eau de vie, sugar syrup and ice in a cocktail shaker and shake vigorously for 1 minute.

2. Put the raspberries in a rocks glass and pour in the cocktail without straining.

3. Top up with chilled mineral water to taste.

187

Blackberry vodka

SERVES: 1 | PREP TIME: 5 MINUTES

INGREDIENTS

6 ice cubes

4 blackberries, washed

2 shots vodka

3 shots lemonade

1 shot blackberry cordial

sprig of mint

METHOD

1. Put the ice cubes and blackberries into the glass and pour in the vodka and lemonade.

2. Pour the cordial down one side of the glass, allowing it to float to the bottom.

3. Serve garnished with a sprig of mint.

Mint marauder

SERVES: 1 | PREP TIME: 5 MINUTES

INGREDIENTS

8-10 mint leaves

1 tsp caster (superfine) sugar

30 ml / 1 fl. oz absinthe

30 ml / 1 fl. oz crème de menthe

½ lemon, juiced

ice

soda water

lemon slices to garnish

METHOD

1. Muddle the mint leaves and sugar in the bottom of a tall glass.

2. Pour the absinthe, crème de menthe and lemon juice before half filling with ice.

3. Stir the ice around the glass to mix the contents and chill the glass.

4. Top up with soda water and garnish with lemon slices.

Cherry bomb

SERVES: 1 | PREP TIME: 5 MINUTES

INGREDIENTS

30 ml / 1 fl. oz vodka

30 ml / 1 fl. oz cherry brandy

1 lime, juiced

ice

cherry juice

lime wedges and cherries to garnish

METHOD

1. Pour the vodka, cherry brandy and lime juice into a cocktail shaker half filled with ice.

2. Shake vigorously for 30 seconds.

3. Strain into a highball glass half filled with ice.

4. Top up with cherry juice and garnish with lime wedges and fresh cherries.

Passion fruit punch

SERVES: 1 | PREP TIME: 5 MINUTES

INGREDIENTS

2 shots passion fruit juice

3 shots white rum

1 shot sugar syrup

1 shot lime juice

6 ice cubes

Prosecco, to top up

1 passion fruit, halved

a few sprigs mint

METHOD

1. Put the passion fruit juice in a cocktail shaker with the rum, sugar syrup, lime juice and ice. Shake vigorously for 1 minute.

2. Strain the cocktail into a tall glass and top up with prosecco.

3. Scoop the passion fruit seeds into the glass and garnish with plenty of mint.

Russian mint

SERVES: 1 | PREP TIME: 10 MINUTES

INGREDIENTS

ice

30 ml / 1 fl. oz espresso vodka

30 ml / 1 fl. oz coffee liqueur

30 ml / 1 fl. oz crème de menthe

1 espresso

200 ml / 7 fl. oz / ¾ cup full fat milk

mint leaves to garnish

METHOD

1. Three quarters fill a blender up with ice and add the vodka, coffee liqueur, crème de menthe and espresso.

2. Blend for 1 minute until smooth and frothy. Add the milk and blend again for 30 seconds.

3. Pour into a tall glass.

4. Top with the mint leaves.

Berry nice

SERVES: 1 | PREP TIME: 5 MINUTES

INGREDIENTS

4 ice cubes

1 shot of cherry liqueur

1 shot of cranberry juice

a pinch of salt

Champagne

TO SERVE:

1 lime slice

a handful of redcurrants

METHOD

1. Put the ice cubes into a cocktail shaker.

2. Pour the cherry liqueur and cranberry juice over the ice cubes in the cocktail shaker, then shake for 10 seconds.

3. Dip the rim of the glass in water, then salt. The salt can be substituted for sugar if a sweeter alternative is desired.

4. Strain the cocktail mixture into a glass and top up with Champagne.

5. Serve garnished with a lime slice and redcurrants.

Strawberries and cream

SERVES: 1 | PREP TIME: 5 MINUTES

INGREDIENTS

ice

30 ml / 1 fl. oz strawberry vodka

30 ml / 1 fl. oz vanilla vodka

300 ml / 10 ½ fl. oz / 1 ¼ cups cream soda

mint leaves and fresh strawberries to garnish

METHOD

1. Half fill a tall glass with ice.

2. Pour the two vodkas over the ice and stir.

3. Top up the glass with the cream soda.

4. Garnish with mint leaves and fresh strawberries.

Tropical crush

SERVES: 1 | PREP TIME: 5 MINUTES

INGREDIENTS

½ fresh watermelon

50 g / 1 ¾ oz frozen pineapple

a handful of mint leaves

1 lemon, juice only

30 ml / 1 fl. oz golden rum

30 ml / 1 fl. oz vodka

ice

METHOD

1. Peel the watermelon and chop the flesh into chunks.

2. Add the ingredients to the cup of a high-powered blender and blend for 45 seconds to 1 minute until smooth.

3. Depending on how thick the drink it, add some ice and blend again to loosen.

4. Pour into a chilled serving glass and garnish with mint.

Cook's Corner

Creative
Mocktails

Virgin berry margarita

SERVES: 2 | PREP TIME: 5 MINUTES

INGREDIENTS

2 tbsp pink sugar crystals

75 g / 2 ½ oz / ½ cup frozen redcurrants,
strawberries and raspberries

250 ml / 9 fl. oz / 1 cup semi-skimmed milk

1 tbsp runny honey

METHOD

1. Moisten the rim of two martini glasses with
water, then dip in the sugar crystals.

2. Put the frozen redcurrants, strawberries,
raspberries, milk and honey in a liquidizer
and blend until very smooth.

3. Divide between the glasses and
serve immediately.

Pink lemon drop

SERVES: 1 | PREP TIME: 5 MINUTES

INGREDIENTS

3 ice cubes

2 shots lemon juice

2 shots lime juice

1 tsp sugar syrup

150 ml / 5 fl. oz pink lemonade

TO SERVE:

1 lemon slice

METHOD

1. Put the ice into a cocktail shaker.

2. Add the lemon juice, lime juice and sugar syrup over the ice in the shaker, then shake for 10 seconds.

3. Pour into a glass and top up with the pink lemonade.

4. Serve immediately with an added lemon slice.

Apple mocktail mule

SERVES: 1 | PREP TIME: 5 MINUTES

INGREDIENTS

3 apples

1 cm ginger

2 shots lime juice

soda water

a handful of ice cubes

1 lime slice

sprig of mint

METHOD

1. Process the apples and ginger through a juicer according to the manufacturer's instructions.

2. Pour the apple and ginger mixture in a glass with the lime juice. Stir well.

3. Top up with soda water then add the ice cubes, lime slice and sprig of mint.

4. Serve immediately.

Berry heaven

SERVES: 1 | PREP TIME: 5 MINUTES

INGREDIENTS

10 frozen raspberries

5 frozen strawberries

5 ice cubes

1 shot pineapple juice, strained

1 shot orange juice, strained

4 shots cranberry juice

3 sprigs of mint

TO SERVE:

extra ice cubes

METHOD

1. Process the raspberries and strawberries through a juicer according to the manufacturer's instructions.

2. Meanwhile, put the ice cubes into a cocktail shaker.

3. Pour the pineapple juice, orange juice, cranberry juice and mint over the ice in the cocktail shaker, then shake for 20 seconds.

4. Strain the mixture from the shaker into a tall glass, leaving the sprigs of mint in the shaker.

5. Add more ice to the glass and serve immediately.

Peach mojito

SERVES: 1 | PREP TIME: 5 MINUTES

●●●●●●●●●●●●●●●●●●●●●●●●●●

INGREDIENTS

1 tbsp mint syrup

2 shots tropical juice

1 tsp sugar

2 shots lime juice

ice cubes

2 peaches, cut into thin wedges

soda water

TO SERVE:

sprig of mint - 1 peach wedge

METHOD

1. Mash the mint syrup, tropical juice and sugar together in a glass.

2. Add the lime juice, ice cubes and peach wedges.

3. Top up with soda water.

4. Serve garnished with a sprig of mint and a wedge of peach.

Tropical hurricane

SERVES: 1 | PREP TIME: 5 MINUTES

●●●●●●●●●●●●●●●●●●●●●●●●●●●

INGREDIENTS

2 handfuls ice cubes

1 shot lime juice

1 shot lemon juice

2 shots passion fruit juice

2 shots pineapple juice, strained

1 shot grenadine

TO SERVE:

2 strawberries, sliced

1 lemon, sliced

2 mint leaves

5 ice cubes

METHOD

1. Put the ice cubes into a cocktail shaker.

2. Pour the lime juice, lemon juice, passion fruit juice, pineapple juice and grenadine over the ice cubes in the cocktail shaker, then shake for 20 seconds.

3. Strain into a glass or jar.

4. Add the sliced strawberries, lemon slices and mint leaves.

5. Serve immediately with more ice cubes.

Chocolate pick me up

SERVES: 2 | PREP TIME: 5 MINUTES

INGREDIENTS

2 tbsp unsweetened cocoa powder

200 ml / 7 fl. oz / ¾ cup semi-skimmed milk

1 tbsp chocolate milkshake powder

2 shots espresso, cooled

8 ice cubes

1 square dark chocolate

METHOD

1. Moisten the rim of two martini glasses with water and dip them in cocoa powder.

2. Put the excess cocoa powder in a cocktail shaker with the milk, milkshake powder, espresso and ice. Shake vigorously for 1 minute, then strain into the glass.

3. Grate the chocolate over the top and serve immediately.

Mango colada

SERVES: 1 | PREP TIME: 5 MINUTES

INGREDIENTS

2 handfuls mango chunks

crushed ice

5 shots pineapple juice

2 shots coconut cream

3 shots mango juice

3 shots tropical juice

TO SERVE:

sprig of mint

METHOD

1. Put the mango chunks and one handful of crushed ice in a blender and whizz for 20 seconds.

2. Put the other handful of crushed ice into the cocktail shaker.

3. Pour the blended mango, pineapple juice and coconut cream over the crushed ice in the shaker and shake for at least 30 seconds.

4. Pour into a glass and top up with the mango juice and tropical juice. Stir well with a cocktail mixer.

5. Serve garnished with a mint sprig.

Tropical mojito

SERVES: 1 | PREP TIME: 5 MINUTES

INGREDIENTS

1 tbsp mint syrup

a handful of pineapple chunks

1 tsp sugar

2 shots lime juice

3 shots pineapple juice

ice cubes

soda water

TO SERVE:

sprig of mint - 2 pineapple chunks

METHOD

1. Mash the mint syrup, pineapple chunks and sugar together in a glass.

2. Add the lime juice, pineapple juice and ice cubes.

3. Top up with soda water.

4. Serve garnished with a sprig of mint and pineapple chunks on a wooden skewer.

Summer tart

SERVES: 1 | PREP TIME: 5 MINUTES

. . . .

INGREDIENTS

5 ice cubes

2 shots lemon juice

150 ml / 5 fl. oz apple juice

½ lemon, cut into wedges

TO SERVE:

6 apple slices

METHOD

1. Put the ice into a cocktail shaker.

2. Add the lemon juice and apple juice over the ice in the shaker, then shake for 20 seconds.

3. Pour into a glass and squeeze the lemon wedges into the mixture to add extra fresh lemon juice.

4. Serve immediately, garnished with apple slices.

Strawberry sling

SERVES: 1 | PREP TIME: 5 MINUTES

●●●●●●●●●●●●●●●●●●●●●●●●

INGREDIENTS

a handful of strawberries, washed

7 ice cubes

2 shots of orange juice

soda water

TO SERVE:

1 orange slice

sprig of mint

METHOD

1. Process the strawberries through a juicer according to the manufacturer's instructions.

2. Meanwhile, put the ice cubes into a cocktail shaker.

3. Add the orange juice over the ice in the shaker, then shake for 10 seconds.

4. Pour into a glass and add the strawberry juice.

5. Top up the mocktail with soda water.

6. Serve with an orange slice and a sprig of mint.

Sunset island

SERVES: 1 | PREP TIME: 5 MINUTES

● ●

INGREDIENTS

3 ice cubes

3 shots pineapple juice

5 shots grapefruit juice

2 tsp sugar syrup

lemonade

TO SERVE:

3 spikes cut from the pineapple crown

3 cm (1 in) orange peel

3 ice cubes

METHOD

1. Put the ice cubes into a cocktail shaker.

2. Pour the pineapple juice, grapefruit juice and sugar syrup over the ice in the cocktail shaker, then shake for 20 seconds.

3. Pour into a tall glass and top up with lemonade.

4. Serve garnished with some spikes cut from the pineapple crown, some orange peel and more ice cubes, if desired.

What-a-ma-ma

SERVES: 1 | PREP TIME: 5 MINUTES

INGREDIENTS

1 tsp sugar syrup

1 tsp mint syrup

1 shot lime juice

1 shot lemon juice

cloudy lemonade, chilled

3 handfuls watermelon chunks

a handful of strawberry chunks

TO SERVE:

sprig of mint

METHOD

1. Pour the sugar syrup, mint syrup, lime juice and lemon juice into the cocktail shaker, then shake for 10 seconds.

2. Strain into a glass or jar and top up with the cloudy lemonade.

3. Add the watermelon and strawberry chunks to the cocktail, stirring well.

4. Serve garnished with a sprig of mint.

Miss Margaret Rita

SERVES: 1 | PREP TIME: 5 MINUTES

INGREDIENTS

3 handfuls crushed ice

2 shots fresh lime juice

3 shots pineapple juice

a pinch of salt

TO SERVE:

1 lime slice

METHOD

1. Put two handfuls of crushed ice into the cocktail shaker.

2. Pour the lime juice and pineapple juice over the crushed ice in the shaker, then shake for 10 seconds.

3. Dip the rim of the margarita glass in water, then salt.

4. Pour the mixture into the glass and add another handful of crushed ice.

5. Serve garnished with a lime slice.

Lime-o-scene

SERVES: 1 | PREP TIME: 5 MINUTES

INGREDIENTS

3 handfuls mint leaves, crushed

1 tsp sugar syrup

2 shots lime juice

1 shot lime cordial

3 shots lemonade

a handful of ice cubes

1 lime, cut into wedges

TO SERVE:

1 lime slice

METHOD

1. Mash the mint leaves and sugar syrup together in a glass.

2. Add in the lime juice, lime cordial and lemonade. Stir well.

3. Add the ice cubes and lime wedges.

4. Serve immediately, garnished with a lime slice.

Raspberry mojito

SERVES: 1 | PREP TIME: 5 MINUTES

INGREDIENTS

2 handfuls raspberries

1 tbsp mint syrup

1 tsp sugar

2 shots lime juice

1 shot apple juice

ice cubes

soda water

TO SERVE:

1 lime slice

a handful of mint leaves

1 raspberry

METHOD

1. Put the raspberries in a blender and whizz for 30 seconds.

2. Meanwhile, mash the mint syrup and sugar together in a glass.

3. Add the lime juice, apple juice, blended raspberries and ice.

4. Top up with soda water.

5. Serve garnished with a lime slice, mint leaves and a raspberry.

INDEX